Workbook for The Psychology of Money

An Unofficial Guide to the Bestselling Book
by Morgan Housel
Jackrabbit Press

CONTENTS

Please Note   1

Introduction   3

1. No One's Crazy   5
    Chapter Summary
    Key Takeaways
    Reflective Questions

2. Luck & Risk   11
    Chapter Summary
    Key Takeaways
    Reflective Questions
    Activity: Mapping Your Luck and Risk

3. Never Enough   18
    Chapter Summary
    Key Takeaways
    Activity: 'Enough' Mind Map
    Reflective Questions

4. Confounding Compounding   22
    Chapter Summary
    Key Takeaways
    Reflective Questions

5. Getting Wealthy vs. Staying Wealthy   27

Chapter Summary
Key Takeaways
Reflective Questions

6. Tails, You Win   32
     Chapter Summary
     Key Takeaways
     Reflective Questions
     Activity: Tail Event Portfolio Simulation
     Tail Event Portfolio Simulation Table

7. Freedom   39
     Chapter Summary
     Key Takeaways
     Reflective Questions
     Activity: Time-Wealth Journal

8. Man in the Car Paradox   45
     Chapter Summary
     Key Takeaways
     Reflective Questions

9. Wealth is What You Don't See   49
     Chapter Summary
     Key Takeaways
     Reflective Questions

10. Save Money   53
     Chapter Summary
     Key Takeaways
     Reflective Questions
     Activity: "Savings Impact Graph"

11. Reasonable > Rational   58

Chapter Summary

Key Takeaways

Activity: Creating a Reflective Decision-Making
Flowchart

12. Surprise!   64

Chapter Summary

Key Takeaways

Reflective Questions

Activity: "The Future Forecast Challenge"

13. Room for Error   69

Chapter Summary

Key Takeaways

Reflective Questions

14. You'll Change   73

Chapter Summary

Key Takeaways

Reflective Questions

Activity: "The Evolving Goals Timeline" Using Online
Tools

15. Nothing's Free   80

Chapter Summary

Key Takeaways

Reflective Questions

16. You & Me   84

Chapter Summary

Key Takeaways

Reflective Questions

17. The Seduction of Pessimism   88

Chapter Summary

Key Takeaways

Reflective Questions

18. When You'll Believe Anything   92

    Chapter Summary

    Key Takeaways

    Reflective Questions

    Activity: Narrative vs. Reality Analysis

19. All Together Now   96

    Chapter Summary

    Key Takeaways

20. Confessions   99

    Chapter Summary

    Key Takeaways

    Reflective Questions

    Activity: Crafting Your Financial Confession - Final
    Workbook Activity

Postscript: A Brief History of Why the U.S. Consumer   106
Thinks the Way They Do

Resources   108

PLEASE NOTE

This workbook is an independent, third-party companion to "The Psychology of Money" by Morgan Housel.

<u>It is not affiliated with, endorsed, or connected to the original author or publisher.</u>

Crafted with original content, this workbook is a distinct entity, free from plagiarism. It is essential to clarify that this is not the original book authored by Morgan Housel. We strongly encourage readers to enrich their experience by obtaining a copy of the original work and offering support and appreciation to the original author.

Please scan the QR code below to be taken to the "The Psychology of Money" purchase page on the Amazon US website:

INTRODUCTION

Welcome to the companion workbook for "The Psychology of Money." This workbook is your guide to deepening your grasp and practical application of the groundbreaking insights found in the original book. Authored by Morgan Housel, "The Psychology of Money" is a seminal work that offers insightful perspectives on how psychological factors drive personal finance more than technical expertise. This workbook aims to honor the integrity and power of the original text while providing an interactive experience to enhance your financial journey.

WHAT'S THIS WORKBOOK ALL ABOUT?

This workbook aligns with the original book's chapters, featuring activities and reflective questions to engage with each concept. It provides space for writing thoughts and reflections, aiding you in better understanding your financial goals. Activities and exercises can empower this process, helping document your reflections and track progress. This workbook is a long-term companion to your financial freedom.

HOW TO USE THIS WORKBOOK

- **Understanding the Core Concepts:** Begin by reading "The Psychology of Money" for foundational knowledge.

- **Chapter Summaries:** Each chapter from the original book is summarized, allowing you to capture the essence of its key messages quickly.

- **Key Takeaways:** At the end of various topics, there

are concise summaries of the main points from the corresponding chapters, designed to refresh your memory and focus your reflections.

- **Reflective Questions and Optional Activities:** The workbook includes thought-provoking questions for deep introspection and the application of the book's principles. Optional activities provide a more immersive experience, but engaging with the reflective questions alone is just as beneficial.

- **Space for Notes:** The workbook offers ample space to jot down your thoughts and plans and track your journey of personal growth.

This workbook aims to provide practical tools that complement the original book and empower you to take concrete steps toward financial control.

Now, let's turn to Chapter One from "The Psychology of Money" and start this journey together...

One

NO ONE'S CRAZY

CHAPTER SUMMARY

Financial perspectives are deeply influenced by one's upbringing, moral values, and economic background. This diversity of experiences leads to varied understandings of how money functions, adding complexity to our grasp of global financial dynamics. Personal financial experiences shape as much as 80% of our thoughts and attitudes toward money, complicating our interpretation of world events. A significant challenge lies in the limitations of research and open-mindedness to fully capture the powerful effects of fear and uncertainty. For instance, perspectives on investment, financial priorities, and risk-taking can significantly differ between those who experienced the Great Depression and those who did not.

Ulrike Malmendier and Stefan Nagel discovered that people's lifelong investment decisions are highly influenced by their own generation's experiences, particularly early in adulthood. Growing up in a period of high inflation or a booming stock market can lead to various financial options, as people may be unaware of the consequences of their choices. Personal history, not intelligence, education, or sophistication, is to blame. For example, a person born in 1970 may have a more significant stock market return or inflation during their adolescence and twenties. In contrast, someone born in 1950 may have a lesser stock market return.

The author contends that people's attitudes toward money are formed by their experiences. They claim that people make decisions based on their existing knowledge and mental picture of the world, which might be inaccurate, partial, or erroneous. The author, for example, uses the example of lottery tickets, which consumers spend more money on than other things. This is frequently due to the misconception that saving is out of reach and that they cannot afford better items. The author contends that this subconscious reasoning is at the root of many financial decisions made at the dinner table or in a business meeting, where personal history, unique worldview, ego, pride, marketing, and odd incentives are scrambled together into a narrative that works for th em.

Due to the topic's relative newness, money judgments are complicated and frequently wrong. The concept of retirement entitlement, which did not emerge until the 1980s, is only two generations old. The 401(k) and Roth IRA were unpopular until 1978 and 1998, respectively. Many Americans are new to retirement savings and investment, as well as index funds, hedge funds, and consumer debt. Our lack of experience and emotion influences our decisions, as we all make them based on our individual experiences. The story of Bill Gates's fortune exemplifies the complexities of financial decisions and the need for a more mature approach.

KEY TAKEAWAYS

1. **Diverse Financial Perspectives**: People's financial behaviors are deeply influenced by their unique backgrounds, including generational experiences, upbringing, economic environments, and personal encounters with risk and reward.

2. **Influence of Personal History**: Individual experiences, more than second-hand knowledge, shape one's financial beliefs and actions.

3. **Generational Impact**: Different economic climates and historical events leave distinct marks on each generation's approach to money.

4. **Relative Nature of Financial Decisions**: What seems irrational or imprudent to one may be perfectly logical to another, given their background and experiences.

5. **Emotional and Psychological Factors**: Personal financial decisions are often more influenced by individual narratives and emotional responses than objective analysis.

REFLECTIVE QUESTIONS

Exploring Personal Financial History: Reflect on a significant financial decision you made in the past. What personal experiences or beliefs influenced this decision?

_____

_____

_____

_____

_____

_____

_____

_____

Generational Financial Perspectives: Consider how your parents or guardians approached money. How has their perspective shaped your financial habits and beliefs?

_____

_____

_____

_____

_____

_____

_____

_____

Economic Climate Influence: Identify a significant financial event during your formative years. How has this event influenced your attitudes toward saving, investing, or spending?

_____

_____

_____

_____

_____

_____

_____

_____

Understanding Others' Financial Choices: Think of someone whose financial decisions seem irrational to you. Given their background and experiences, can you empathize with their perspective?

_____

_____

_____

_____

_____

_____

_____

_____

Two

Luck & Risk

Chapter Summary

Chapter Two examines how outcomes in life are influenced by factors beyond individual effort, highlighting the intertwined nature of luck and risk. It uses Bill Gates' story to illustrate this concept. Gates attended Lakeside School, one of the few high schools at the time with a computer, where he and classmate Paul Allen honed their computer skills. This opportunity, available to only 300 students at Lakeside, gave Gates a significant advantage and a unique perspective on computers that many seasoned professionals lacked.

The chapter contrasts Gates' success with the story of Kent Evans, a talented peer whose potential was tragically cut short by a mountaineering accident before finishing high school. Evans' story exemplifies how chance and risk play unpredictable roles in life's outcomes. For every success story like Bill Gates, there is someone like Kent Evans, equally talented and driven yet ultimately shaped by the unpredictability of life.

The chapter asserts that luck and risk are critical factors in life's outcomes, often overlooked due to their intangible nature. Financial success is not always an accurate reflection of individual effort. Acknowledging the role of luck can be perceived as dismissive while focusing solely on risk can be demoralizing. The difficulty lies in distinguishing between calculated and risky decisions, and it's often easier to rationalize past choices than to confront personal shortcomings.

Morgan Housel discusses the complexities of understanding money and investment. He suggests that quick fixes are often sought, ignoring more intricate aspects. The chapter references Cornelius Vanderbilt and John D. Rockefeller, indicating that their entrepreneurial success was not solely due to luck or inherent skill. Housel emphasizes the importance of learning from both successes and failures, recognizing the role of leverage, effective leadership, and customer insight in business.

The chapter concludes that recognizing the duality of risk and chance is challenging. Instead of focusing on extreme cases, it advises looking at broader patterns of success and failure. Success can be misleading, leading competent individuals to overestimate their invincibility. Similarly, risk can abruptly change fortunes. Effective management of failure involves structuring one's financial life to withstand poor investments and missed goals. In evaluating failures, self-forgiveness and understanding are essential. The chapter reminds readers that situations are seldom as straightforward as they seem, either for better or worse.

KEY TAKEAWAYS

1. **Siblings of Chance**: Luck and risk are presented as interconnected forces, both playing significant roles in the outcomes of various endeavors.

2. **Case of Bill Gates**: Gates' success is partly attributed to his unique opportunity to access advanced computing in high school, highlighting the impact of luck.

3. **The Other Side of Fortune**: The story of Kent Evans, Gates' friend who died young, showcases the harsh realities of risk.

4. **The Complexity of Judging Success**: The difficulty separating skill, luck, and risk when evaluating financial outcomes and the dangers of misattributing success solely to individual efforts.

5. **Broad Patterns Over Individual Cases**: Emphasizing learning from general trends and patterns rather than focusing solely on extreme or individual cases is essential for one's growth.

REFLECTIVE QUESTIONS

Evaluating Others' Success: Consider someone you know who is very successful. How much of their success would you attribute to luck? Does this change how you view their achievements?

Learning from Patterns vs. Individual Stories: Can you think of a broad financial pattern or trend you have observed that offers a more reliable lesson than an individual success or failure story? How has this pattern influenced your financial thinking?

ACTIVITY: MAPPING YOUR LUCK AND RISK

Objective

To visually explore and understand the roles of luck and risk in your personal and financial life. This activity will help you identify how external factors have influenced your successes and challenges.

Instructions

1. **Create a Luck-Risk Axis**: Draw a large cross on your paper, creating four quadrants. Label the horizontal axis "Luck" (negative luck on the left, positive luck on the right) and the vertical axis "Risk" (low risk at the bottom, high risk at the top).

2. **Identify Key Events**:

   - Think of significant events in your life, particularly those related to financial decisions, career moves, or personal achievements.

   - Include both successes and failures.

3. **Plot the Events**:

   - For each event, decide where it falls on the Luck-Risk Axis. Was the event more influenced by luck or by your own decisions? Was it a high-risk or low-risk situation?

   - Plot these events on the graph accordingly. Use different colors or symbols for successes and failures.

4. **Analyze Patterns**: Look for patterns in your graph. Do you tend to have more success in high-risk situations, or do you thrive in low-risk environments? How much has luck

influenced your life?

5. **Reflective Questions**:

   ○ After completing your map, reflect on the following questions:

     • How does visualizing these events change your perception of luck and risk in your life?

     • Are there any lessons you can learn about how you handle risk or how you respond to luck?

     • How might this understanding influence your future decisions?

Conclusion

This activity aims to provide a visual and reflective understanding of how luck and risk have played roles in your life. It encourages a balanced view of success and failure, considering external factors beyond personal control.

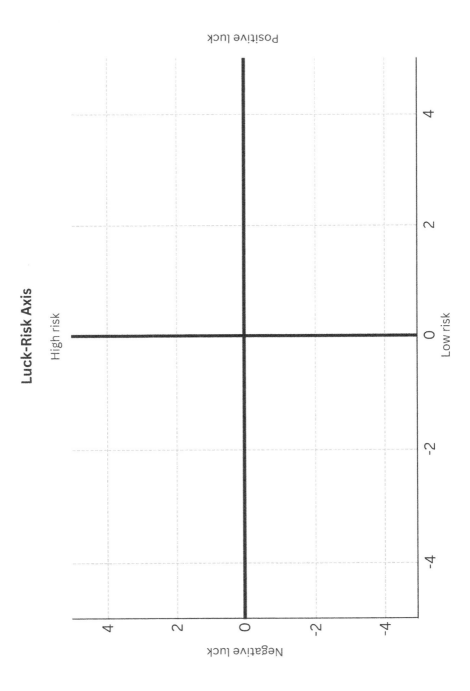

Three

NEVER ENOUGH

CHAPTER SUMMARY

John Bogle, the founder of Vanguard, often emphasized the importance of understanding what constitutes 'enough' in the context of wealth. He highlighted the ever-expanding nature of this concept, which is both insightful and significant. Bogle's perspective gains relevance when considering the cases of Rajat Gupta and Bernie Madoff, who fell into the trap of never having enough. Gupta, hailing from Kolkata, made his way up in McKinsey and Goldman Sachs. Despite his considerable achievements, his aspiration to amass billionaire status led him to engage in a side business. His involvement in insider trading, particularly around the time Warren Buffett invested $5 billion in Goldman Sachs during the 2008 financial crisis, resulted in imprisonment for both Gupta and Raj Rajaratnam, devastating their careers and reputations.

Similarly, Bernie Madoff, infamous for orchestrating a massive Ponzi scheme, was a legitimate market maker before his downfall. His scheme, which promised substantial returns, led to losses amounting to billions, showcasing the dangers of greed. Madoff's earnings as a market maker, which ranged between $25 and $50 million annually, were overshadowed by his fraudulent activities.

Both Gupta and Madoff exemplify how the lack of sufficiency can lead to the squandering of wealth, respect, power, and freedom. This phenomenon is not exclusive to criminal activities. It is also seen in non-criminal instances like the collapse of the hedge fund

Long-Term Capital Management, which took excessive risks to pursue more, ultimately leading to its downfall.

Bogle's assertion underlines the perils of chasing an unattainable social comparison ceiling, suggesting that the relentless pursuit of more can lead to regret. He argues that the true essence of life lies in recognizing the value of sufficiency. Acknowledging the worth of reputation, freedom, independence, family, friends, and happiness and knowing when to cease taking risks that could jeopardize these invaluable aspects of life is fundamental. This understanding is not about being conservative but realizing that an insatiable desire for more often leads to regrettable outcomes.

KEY TAKEAWAYS

1. **The Elegance of 'Enough'**: The concept of 'enough' represents a critical yet often overlooked aspect of financial satisfaction and personal fulfillment.

2. **Dangers of Excess**: The stories of Rajat Gupta and Bernie Madoff exemplify how the insatiable pursuit of wealth can lead to ruinous consequences.

3. **Comparative Wealth**: The endless comparison with others' wealth and success often fuels dissatisfaction and the relentless pursuit of more.

4. **Personal Wealth Goals**: Recognizing and appreciating what one has is essential in avoiding the pitfalls of uncontrolled ambition and risk.

5. **Value Beyond Wealth**: The chapter reiterates the importance of non-monetary values like reputation, relationships, and personal happiness.

Activity: 'Enough' Mind Map

- Create a mind map centered around the word "Enough." Branch out with factors like personal values, financial goals, fears, and influences.

- This visual exercise will help you explore what 'enough' encompasses in your life beyond just monetary value.

Enough

REFLECTIVE QUESTIONS

Lessons from Stories of Excess: Considering the stories of Gupta and Madoff, what lessons can you draw about the risks of excessive wealth pursuit?

_____

_____

_____

_____

_____

_____

_____

_____

Reevaluating Financial Goals: Reflect on your current financial goals. Are they driven by a sense of necessity, ambition, or comparison with others?

_____

_____

_____

_____

_____

_____

_____

_____

Four

Confounding Compounding

Chapter Summary

The history of ice ages, spanning several billion years, demonstrates that Earth has gone through multiple freezing and thawing cycles. These cycles are influenced by the gravitational forces of the sun and moon, which affect Earth's orbit and axial tilt, thereby contributing to climatic changes. An ice age cycle typically commences when the summer heat fails to melt the previous winter's snow completely. This residual snow sets the stage for more accumulation in subsequent winters. Gradually, this process leads to the formation of massive continental ice sheets. A critical takeaway from the study of ice ages is how minor shifts in conditions can precipitate dramatic environmental transformations. This concept of incremental change leading to significant outcomes is paralleled in finance.

Warren Buffett's financial success, for instance, can be largely attributed to the financial foundation he established during his youth and the long-term commitment he maintained through his adult years. The principle of compounding has been central to Buffett's wealth accumulation. Contrary to the claim that if Buffett had continued compounding at 22% annually, his net worth today would be $11.9 million, the impact of such a rate over his investing career would be significantly higher. Buffett's investment expertise is well-recognized, but it's the prolonged duration of his investments that has been pivotal.

Comparatively, hedge fund manager Jim Simons, who has achieved an average annual return of 66% since 1988, has amassed a substantial fortune yet remains less wealthy than Buffett. This discrepancy is a testament to the power of time in the compounding equation. Simons' shorter investment timeframe compared to Buffett's longer one illustrates why Buffett's net worth surpasses Simons's despite the latter's higher annual returns.

This highlights an essential lesson in investing: it's about achieving high returns and sustaining good returns over an extended period. The nature of compounding can sometimes lead to unexpected outcomes, including disappointing trades or flawed strategies. However, the key to successful investing lies in generating consistent returns over the longest time rather than aiming for the highest returns in the short term.

Key Takeaways

1. **Historical Understanding of Earth**: The discovery of Earth's ice ages provided significant insights into its history and the forces shaping it.

2. **Milanković's Theory**: Milutin Milanković's theory showed how Earth's tilt and orbit lead to cycles of ice ages, emphasizing the impact of small changes over time.

3. **Compounding in Nature**: The gradual buildup of snow leading to ice ages illustrates how small, consistent changes can lead to significant outcomes.

4. **Warren Buffett's Wealth**: Buffett's fortune exemplifies the power of compounding in finance, where consistent, long-term investment leads to extraordinary wealth.

5. **Compounding in Technology**: The exponential growth in technology, particularly in data storage, demonstrates how compounding can lead to unimaginable progress.

REFLECTIVE QUESTIONS

Small Changes, Big Impact:

- Think about a small habit or action you've maintained over time. How has this compounded over time to impact your life significantly?

- Reflect on how this principle of compounding could be applied to other areas of your life.

Financial Growth Reflection:

- Consider your own financial habits. What small, consistent actions could you take that might compound over time to improve your financial health?

- How does the concept of compounding influence your perspective on long-term financial planning?

Five

GETTING WEALTHY VS. STAYING WEALTHY

CHAPTER SUMMARY

Following the stock market crash of 1929, Jesse Livermore, a notable figure in the world of trading, emerged as one of the wealthiest individuals of his time. However, the reality was more nuanced. While Livermore profited by shorting the market, his wife Dorothy was distressed upon learning about his speculative methods. Although Livermore gained considerable wealth, the amount of over $3 billion mentioned seems inflated when considering historical records.

Similarly, Abraham Germansky, a real estate developer who had amassed a fortune in the 1920s, faced ruin due to the 1929 crash. Livermore, too, experienced a dramatic reversal of fortune. His initial success led to overconfidence, and he eventually lost his wealth in the stock market. In 1933, Livermore disappeared for two days, marking a significant downturn in his life. Both Livermore and Germansky exemplified a familiar pattern: while adept at acquiring wealth, they struggled to maintain it. This underscores a fundamental challenge in capitalism: the skills required to make money differ significantly from those needed to keep it.

The key to success in investment, career, or business is often survival. This means enduring over time without being forced to quit, which is essential for the power of compounding to take effect. Rarely are short-term gains so critical that they justify risking everything. Compounding is effective only when an asset has the opportunity to grow over time and can weather unexpected fluctuations.

This principle can be seen in the careers of investors like Warren Buffett and Charlie Munger. Another associate, Rick Guerin, also achieved considerable success but faced setbacks due to over-leveraging. Embracing a survival mindset involves recognizing the importance of being financially resilient, owning appreciating assets, and understanding the power of compounding. The most impressive returns are those that are sustained over the longest periods.

While planning is crucial, preparing for plans not unfolding as expected is equally essential. A robust plan accommodates unpredictability and includes flexibility. In finance, the concept of a margin of safety—enhancing the likelihood of success at a given risk level—is often overlooked but highly impactful. Adopting a 'barbell personality' is beneficial: be optimistic about the future but cautious about the obstacles that might prevent you from reaching it. This form of sensible optimism acknowledges that while the long-term outlook may be favorable, short-term challenges are inevitable.

Jesse Livermore's story is a testament to this mindset. He recognized that good times often follow bad and believed that learning from one's experiences, no matter the cost, is invaluable. This philosophy highlights the importance of resilience and learning in the journey of financial success.

KEY TAKEAWAYS

1. **The Dual Nature of Wealth Management**: Achieving financial success requires the skill to acquire wealth through risks and optimism and the discipline to maintain it through frugality and an awareness of the role of luck.

2. **Historical Lessons on Wealth**: Jesse Livermore and Abraham Germansky's stories illustrate wealth's volatility and the consequences of failing to balance acquisition with preservation.

3. **Importance of a Survival Mindset**: The key to long-term financial stability is not just growth or intelligence but the ability to survive over time. This survival mindset involves planning for uncertainties and having a margin of safety.

4. **Compounding and Longevity**: The power of compounding is most effective when there is a consistent approach over a long period. Survival through various market cycles is crucial for compounding to work its wonders.

5. **Balanced Personality for Financial Success**: A successful financial mindset requires being optimistic about future growth and paranoid about potential risks and challenges. This balance enables one to navigate uncertainties without losing sight of long-term goals.

REFLECTIVE QUESTIONS

Contrasting Financial Strategies:

1. Reflect on your approach to financial management. How do you balance the pursuit of wealth (taking risks, being optimistic) with the need to preserve it (being frugal, recognizing the role of luck)?

2. Consider a financial decision you made in the past. How did this decision reflect a balance (or imbalance) between these two aspects?

Learning from Historical Examples:

- Think about the stories of Jesse Livermore and Abraham Germansky. Which aspects of their financial journeys resonate with your own experiences or fears about wealth management?

- How might their stories influence your future financial decisions?

Six

TAILS, YOU WIN

CHAPTER SUMMARY

In 2000, renowned art dealer Heinz Berggruen made a notable deal by selling to the German government a significant collection of artworks by Picasso, Braque, Klee, and Matisse. The transaction, reportedly valued at a fraction of its estimated market value, underscores the subjective nature of art valuation. This sale exemplifies how art investors often gather diverse portfolios, awaiting a few pieces to appreciate in value significantly. This concept mirrors the 'long tail' phenomenon in business and finance, where a small number of successes can outweigh many failures or moderate outcomes.

For instance, Walt Disney's early triumph with "Snow White and the Seven Dwarfs" was a pivotal 'tail event' that transformed the fortunes of Disney Studios. Such tail events are especially crucial in industries like venture capital, where the majority of investments might not yield high returns, but a few successful ones can be extraordinarily lucrative.

The same principle can be observed in the broader stock market. For example, the performance of large public equities often shows a similar pattern to venture capital: many companies underperform, some do moderately well, and a few achieve exceptional success, driving most of the market's gains. Reflecting on the Russell 3000 Index, it's notable that while there is a significant failure rate, a few companies have contributed disproportionately to the market's overall returns. For instance, in specific years like 2018, companies like Amazon and Apple significantly impacted the S&P 500's returns, mainly through successful ventures like Amazon Prime, Amazon Web Services, and Apple's iPhone.

This pattern of a few key factors driving the majority of outcomes applies to companies and personal investment strategies. An investor's success is often defined by their responses to short-term challenges rather than long-term passive strategies.

In business, investing, and finance, 'tail events' can dominate outcomes. Many attempts may lead to failure or modest success, but the rare, significant success often defines a career or a company. This concept contrasts with fields where decisions consistently yield predictable results. The path to remarkable achievements in these sectors is usually lined with failures and setbacks, barely visible in the final successful outcome. The career of someone like Chris Rock in comedy is a testament to this; behind the visible success are countless trials and errors, emphasizing that our missteps and setbacks are often just as influential as our successes.

KEY TAKEAWAYS

1. **The Rarity of Massive Success**: Exceptional success, whether in art collection, business, or investing, often comes from a small percentage of highly successful endeavors amidst a majority of average or failed ones.

2. **Importance of Diverse Endeavors**: Success stories like Berggruen's art collection show that casting a wide net and embracing various opportunities can lead to significant outcomes, even if many attempts do not yield results.

3. **The Role of Persistence and Resilience**: Examples from Disney's early struggles to later triumphs emphasize the importance of perseverance and learning from failures.

4. **Long-Tail Dynamics in Investing**: The disproportionate impact of a few successful investments in a portfolio highlights the importance of recognizing and capitalizing on tail events.

5. **Adapting to Uncertainty**: The concept of being right only a fraction of the time but still achieving success underlines the need for flexibility and adaptation in uncertain environments.

REFLECTIVE QUESTIONS

Assessing Your Own Tail Events: Reflect on your personal or professional life. Can you identify any 'tail events' that have significantly influenced your journey? How did these moments shape your path?

_____

_____

_____

_____

_____

_____

_____

Learning from Failures: Consider a time when you faced failure or a setback. How did this experience contribute to your growth or lead to a future success akin to a tail event?

_____

_____

_____

_____

_____

_____

ACTIVITY: TAIL EVENT PORTFOLIO SIMULATION

Objective

Create a simulated portfolio to explore tail events in investing, mirroring the principles discussed in the chapter. This exercise illustrates how a diverse portfolio can lead to significant outcomes, emphasizing the impact of rare but high-return investments.

Instructions

1. **Create a Simulated Investment Portfolio**:

   - Develop a list of up to 12 hypothetical investments. These can represent various sectors, industries, or types of business ventures.

   - Assign a fictional budget and distribute it across these investments. Not all investments need to receive the same amount, reflecting real-world diversification strategies.

2. **Research and Decide Outcomes**:

   - For each investment, research real-world equivalents or use your imagination to decide its fate: successful, failed, or moderately successful.

   - Determine the return for each successful investment and the loss for each failure.

3. **Calculate Overall Portfolio Performance**: After assigning outcomes to each investment, calculate the overall return of your portfolio. This will help you understand how just a few successful investments can offset multiple failures.

4. **Reflection and Analysis**:

- Reflect on the distribution of your investments and their outcomes. Which types of investments yielded the highest returns? Were there patterns in the failures?

- Consider how this exercise relates to tail events in investing and business. What insights can you draw about risk-taking and diversification?

Materials Needed

- The spreadsheet on the next page and a pen or a digital spreadsheet for recording and calculations.

- Access to research materials for investment ideas and outcomes (optional).

Purpose

This activity offers a hands-on understanding of how tail events operate in investment portfolios. It aims to demonstrate the significance of diversification and the acceptance of failures as part of a successful overall strategy, aligning with the chapter's key themes.

Tail Event Portfolio Simulation Table

Investment	Allocated Budget ($)	Type	Outcome	Return/Loss (%)
Example: Investment 1	*1000*	*Tech*	*TBD*	*TBD*

Seven

FREEDOM

CHAPTER SUMMARY

Achieving control over one's life is a pinnacle form of wealth and a significant predictor of happiness. The common aspiration for wealth is often rooted in the pursuit of happiness. Money's greatest intrinsic value lies in its ability to grant control over time, leading to independence and autonomy through financial security. Investing money in creating time and options offers a lifestyle advantage unparalleled by most luxury items. Strategically allocating funds towards a life that allows freedom of choice in activities, companions, location, and duration can yield substantial returns in personal satisfaction.

Despite being the world's wealthiest country, the United States has not seen a marked increase in happiness among its population since the 1950s. Economic growth has allowed for the acquisition of superior goods and a lifestyle that would have been inconceivable for a middle-class family in the 1950s. For example, the average size of American homes has expanded significantly, from 983 square feet in 1950 to 2,436 square feet in 2018, often featuring more bathrooms than occupants. However, this material growth has not necessarily translated into greater personal autonomy. The nature of contemporary occupations often results in less control over one's time. Today, a significant portion of the workforce is engaged in managerial, official, or professional roles alongside a large service sector. These job types can blur the boundaries between work and personal life, creating a perception of continuous work, particularly in roles that involve consistent mental engagement.

Addressing this challenge involves recognizing and valuing elements that universally contribute to happiness. These include nurturing strong friendships, being part of something larger than oneself, and enjoying quality, unstructured time with family. Acknowledging the importance of these aspects can help balance the pursuit of material wealth with the pursuit of a fulfilling and happy life.

KEY TAKEAWAYS

1. **Wealth as a Means to Control:** The highest form of wealth is the ability to decide what to do with your time, emphasizing autonomy over daily choices as a critical driver of happiness.

2. **Psychological Perspective on Happiness:** Angus Campbell's research indicates that a sense of control over one's life is a stronger predictor of wellbeing than traditional measures of success, like income or job prestige.

3. **Intrinsic Value of Money:** Money's greatest value lies in its ability to grant independence and autonomy, not in the material goods it can buy.

4. **Impact of Modern Work on Time Control:** The nature of contemporary jobs, often requiring constant mental engagement, has changed the dynamic of work-life balance, highlighting the challenge of maintaining control over one's time in the digital age.

5. **Elderly Wisdom on Happiness:** Insights from elderly individuals emphasize the importance of relationships, experiences, and unstructured time with loved ones over material wealth.

REFLECTIVE QUESTIONS

Personal Definition of Wealth:

- Reflect on your own definition of wealth. How much does the ability to control your time and decisions factor into this definition?

- Can you think of a moment when you felt genuinely wealthy, not in financial terms, but in your ability to choose how you spent your time?

Evaluating Life Choices:

- Consider the decisions you've made in pursuit of happiness and wealth. Have these decisions increased your sense of autonomy and control over your life?

- How might you adjust your future choices to align more closely with the idea that true wealth lies in controlling your time?

ACTIVITY: TIME-WEALTH JOURNAL

Objective

Create a journal to track and reflect on how you spend your time over a week, relating it to your sense of autonomy and happiness.

Instructions

1. **Daily Time Tracking**: For one week, keep a detailed journal of how you spend your time each day. Include work, leisure, family time, and any other significant activities.

2. **Reflections on Autonomy**: At the end of each day, reflect on the moments when you felt you had control over your time versus when you felt controlled by external obligations.

3. **Happiness Correlation**: Note any patterns you observe between your sense of autonomy and your overall mood or purpose of fulfillment.

4. **Weekly Review**: At the end of the week, review your journal. Identify activities that contributed most to your happiness and those that detracted from it.

Purpose

This activity is designed to help you understand how your time management correlates with your sense of wealth and happiness. It encourages a deeper understanding of the value of autonomy in daily life and helps identify areas for potential change to enhance overall wellbeing.

Eight

MAN IN THE CAR PARADOX

CHAPTER SUMMARY

This short chapter offers an introspective look at the pursuit of wealth and luxury, particularly through the lens of a valet's experience with high-end cars and their owners. It challenges the common perception that material possessions automatically confer respect and admiration.

KEY TAKEAWAYS

1. **Misconception of Material Wealth**: Owning luxury items like expensive cars is often seen as a symbol of success and a means to garner admiration and respect from others. However, this perception is frequently misguided.

2. **The Driver vs. The Car Paradox**: The allure of luxury items often overshadows the individual owning them. People are more likely to envy the item (like a Ferrari) rather than respect the person owning it.

3. **Desire for Admiration**: The underlying motivation for acquiring expensive possessions is often the desire for admiration and respect from others, but this strategy rarely achieves the intended emotional fulfillment.

4. **The True Path to Respect**: Gaining genuine respect and admiration is less about displaying wealth and more about personal qualities like humility, kindness, and empathy.

5. **Reevaluating Wealth Goals**: The chapter encourages reevaluating why one seeks wealth and luxury. It suggests that while there's nothing wrong with pursuing wealth or fancy cars, understanding the real reasons behind these desires is crucial.

REFLECTIVE QUESTIONS

Personal Perception of Wealth:

- Reflect on how you perceive people who own luxury items. Do you find yourself admiring the person, or are you more impressed by their possessions?

- How does this perception influence your own aspirations for wealth and luxury items?

True Sources of Admiration:

- Think about someone you genuinely admire and respect. What qualities do they possess that earn your admiration? Are these qualities related to their wealth or material possessions?

- How might this insight shape your own goals and actions in pursuit of respect and admiration?

Nine

WEALTH IS WHAT YOU DON'T SEE

CHAPTER SUMMARY

Wealth is often misconceived as material possessions, yet its true essence lies in the unseen. In the mid-2000s, the ownership of a Ferrari was commonly perceived as a symbol of affluence, emphasizing the importance of appearances over actual wealth. However, this perspective can be misleading. There are numerous instances where individuals with moderate success spend a significant portion of their income on luxury cars, creating an imaginary image of financial prosperity. True wealth isn't just about the expensive cars not bought; it also involves accumulating financial assets that remain unconverted into physical possessions.

Modern capitalism sometimes projects an illusion of wealth, making it seem like an easily attainable goal. However, genuine wealth is not about the expenditure on material items but rather the prudence to refrain from unnecessary spending. Financial commentator Bill Mann aptly stated that the path to wealth involves spending within one's means rather than beyond them. This principle not only facilitates wealth accumulation but also fundamentally defines it.

Wealth extends beyond current income; it encompasses the potential to afford future purchases, offering the flexibility and capacity to acquire more than one can currently afford. Because wealth is often discreet, finding wealthy role models can be challenging as their assets are not always visible. It's common to see wealthy individuals making significant purchases, but their hidden financial reserves truly define their wealth. The desire to attain wealth is widespread, yet there's a pervasive misconception that possessing money necessitates spending it. This misunderstanding overlooks the restraint necessary for true financial success.

The inconspicuous nature of real wealth complicates the task of emulation and learning. The world is replete with individuals who may seem modest but possess substantial wealth and those who appear affluent but are close to insolvency. An essential principle to remember is that wealth is characterized by avoided expenses, underscoring the importance of saving over spending.

KEY TAKEAWAYS

1. **Wealth vs. Appearance**: Wealth is not about the conspicuous display of luxury items but rather the accumulation and preservation of financial assets that aren't immediately visible.

2. **Misinterpretation of Richness**: People often mistake possessing expensive items as an indication of wealth, overlooking that such displays often reflect spent income or debt.

3. **Wealth as Hidden Security**: True wealth provides options, flexibility, and the ability to make future purchases, contrasting with the immediate gratification of spending on luxury.

4. **The Paradox of Saving and Spending**: The essence of wealth lies in the restraint of not spending rather than the capacity to spend.

5. **Learning from the Unseen**: The hidden nature of wealth makes it difficult to understand and imitate, as the most financially successful individuals often do not display their wealth overtly.

REFLECTIVE QUESTIONS

Understanding Personal Wealth Perceptions: How does your perception of wealth align with the idea that true wealth is what isn't seen? Have you ever misjudged someone's financial status based on their outward appearance?

_____

_____

_____

_____

_____

_____

_____

Reassessing Financial Goals: Reflect on your own financial goals. Are they more aligned with acquiring visible symbols of wealth or building unseen financial security? How might this understanding change your approach to wealth?

_____

_____

_____

_____

_____

_____

_____

Ten

SAVE MONEY

CHAPTER SUMMARY

Chapter 10 discusses the significance of saving money and its role in personal financial success. Morgan Housel argues that wealth accumulation is less about income or investment returns and more about the saving rate. While energy efficiency is largely controllable, personal savings and frugality often present a more significant challenge.

Accumulating wealth typically requires more money or higher investment returns, yet controlling one's savings rate is crucial. Wealth, in essence, is the balance remaining after expenses. A high savings rate is pivotal, as without it, the potential to generate wealth is limited, irrespective of income. The actual value of wealth is relative to individual needs, and finding contentment with less can significantly widen the gap between desires and possessions.

A high savings rate indicates the ability to live below one's means, allowing savings to extend further than with higher spending. This underscores the importance of focusing on savings over simply earning more. It's observed that people with substantial incomes often save little, as their ego influences their spending. Individuals can enhance their savings and secure their financial future by defining savings as the difference between ego and income. Those who achieve sustained personal finance success often do so by ignoring societal pressures, which in turn makes saving an achievable goal.

Reducing expenditure and being indifferent to others' perceptions can significantly aid in saving money. Money management is more psychological than financial, and saving doesn't necessarily need a specific goal. Saving without a defined spending objective offers flexibility and the ability to adapt as circumstances change. This approach can yield unexpected returns on wealth, providing opportunities that might otherwise be missed.

In the modern, hyper-connected world, the competition in the job market has expanded dramatically from local to global scales. This shift is particularly evident in professions that prioritize intellectual over physical skills. Standing out in an increasingly competitive environment becomes essential. In an era where many technical skills are automated and intellectual prowess alone doesn't guarantee success, flexibility is becoming a highly valued asset.

Control over one's time and options is emerging as a critical factor in today's economy. Therefore, more people should focus on saving, adopting a less rigid financial approach.

KEY TAKEAWAYS

1. **Savings Rate Over Income**: Building wealth is less about the amount of income or investment returns and more about the rate at which you save and manage your expenses.

2. **Efficiency in Wealth Building**: The analogy of energy efficiency is used to illustrate how managing and reducing what you need can be more impactful than increasing what you have.

3. **The Illusion of High Income**: A high income does not necessarily equate to wealth; true wealth is often hidden in savings and investments.

4. **The Power of Frugality**: Embracing a frugal lifestyle and focusing on saving can lead to greater financial security than solely seeking high investment returns.

5. **Flexibility and Control**: Savings provide flexibility, control over time, and the ability to withstand life's surprises, highlighting the unseen benefits of having a solid financial buffer.

REFLECTIVE QUESTIONS

Personal Savings Philosophy: How do you prioritize saving in your financial life? Do you focus more on earning more or saving more, and why?

_____

_____

_____

_____

_____

_____

_____

Redefining Wealth:

- How does the chapter's perspective on wealth as "unseen" savings alter your view of financial success?

- Consider how this understanding might change your financial behaviors or goals.

_____

_____

_____

_____

_____

_____

_____

ACTIVITY: "SAVINGS IMPACT GRAPH"

Objective

Create a graph to visualize the impact of savings on your long-term financial health, highlighting the power of compounding and efficiency.

Instructions

1. **Graph Setup**: On graph paper or a digital graphing tool, create a graph with time on the x-axis and total financial assets on the y-axis.

2. **Plot Two Scenarios**: Plot two lines - one representing your financial growth with your current savings rate and another with an increased savings rate.

3. **Analyze Compounding Effect**: Observe the divergence of the two lines over time to understand the compounding effect of increased savings.

4. **Reflect on Changes**: Based on your graph, reflect on potential changes you could make in your savings habits and how they could impact your long-term financial health.

Purpose

This activity is designed to provide a clear visual representation of how incremental changes in your savings rate can significantly impact your financial future. It emphasizes the importance of savings and frugality in wealth accumulation.

Eleven

REASONABLE > RATIONAL

CHAPTER SUMMARY

In this chapter, Housel focuses on the importance of prudent financial decision-making. He references Julius Wagner-Jauregg, a psychiatrist from the late 19th century who made a significant discovery regarding neurosyphilis treatment. Wagner-Jauregg observed that patients suffering from severe neurosyphilis showed improvement when they experienced high fevers from other illnesses. To leverage this, he introduced "malariotherapy," where he injected patients with malaria to induce fever, which, in turn, helped combat syphilis. After extensive experimentation, he found that this method aided the recovery of 6 out of 10 neurosyphilis patients, a notable improvement compared to the 3 out of 10 recovery rate in untreated patients. Housel draws a parallel to this medical approach, suggesting that fevers, often seen as mere annoyances, play a critical role in bodily recovery.

Extending this analogy to financial decision-making, Housel argues that being reasonable is often more beneficial than being purely rational. He brings up Harry Markowitz, a Nobel Prize-winning economist known for his work on balancing risk and reward in investments. Housel highlights that investing has a social aspect often neglected when viewed solely from a financial perspective.

A 2008 Yale study is cited, recommending that young investors should favor stocks at a two-to-one margin. This approach allows them to take on more risk in their youth and navigate the volatile market effectively. However, while mathematically sound, Housel points out that this strategy might not be practical in the long term. He advocates for an emotional connection to investments, arguing that a lack of emotional investment can increase the likelihood of abandoning strategies, making rational thinking potentially disadvantageous. Staying committed to an investment strategy during tough times can offer tangible benefits, as passionate investors are more likely to persist through challenges.

Finally, Housel addresses the idea of home bias in investments, where individuals prefer investing in domestic companies. He contrasts this with day trading and selecting individual stocks in small quantities, suggesting that these practices can be rational if they fulfill specific psychological needs, even if they don't align with traditional investment wisdom.

KEY TAKEAWAYS

1. **Reasonable vs. Rational**: Rational financial decisions are often idealized but can be impractical in real-life scenarios. Aiming for reasonableness in financial choices aligns better with human nature and behavior.

2. **Emotional Connection to Investments**: Developing an emotional attachment to investments can be beneficial, as it increases the likelihood of staying committed during challenging periods.

3. **Importance of Personal Satisfaction**: Financial strategies should be about maximizing returns and finding personal satisfaction and comfort in financial decisions.

4. **Home Bias in Investing**: While not entirely rational, preferring domestic investments due to familiarity can be reasonable if it helps maintain a consistent investment strategy.

5. **Accepting Imperfection**: Understanding and accepting that financial decisions won't always be perfect or rational can lead to more sustainable and long-term financial.

ACTIVITY: CREATING A REFLECTIVE DECISION-MAKING FLOWCHART

Overview

This activity involves creating a Reflective Decision-Making Flowchart to track and analyze your financial decisions visually. This tool will help you understand the interplay between emotional and rational factors in your decision-making process and plan better for future financial choices.

Materials Needed

- Paper or a digital tool for drawing (like Microsoft Visio, Lucidchart, or a simple drawing app).

- A list of recent financial decisions for reflection.

Instructions

1. **Identify a Recent Financial Decision**: Choose a recent financial decision you made. This could be an investment, a significant purchase, a savings plan, or any other financial choice.

2. **Set Up Your Flowchart**: Draw a large box at the top of your paper or screen. Label it with the financial decision you've chosen.

3. **Branch Out for Factors**:

   ○ Draw two branching paths from your decision box. Label one path "Emotional Factors" and the other "Rational Factors. "Add smaller boxes or bubbles in each path and fill them with the specific emotional and rational factors that influenced your decision. For example, under "Emotional Factors," you might write "excitement about potential gains" or "fear of loss."

4. **Converge to Decision Made**: Where the paths converge, draw a box labeled "Decision Mad.". Write a brief description of what decision you ultimately made.

5. **Outcome Section**: Below the "Decision Made" box, add another labeled "Outcom.". Here, write the result or the current status of the decision.

6. **Reflective Analysis**:

   ○ Add a section for reflection. Ask yourself:

     • Did emotional or rational factors play a larger role in my decision?

     • Was the outcome affected by the balance of these factors?

     • Could a different approach have led to a better result?

7. **Plan Future Strategies**:

   ○ Create a section labeled "Future Approach Strate based on your reflection.". Here, outline how you might approach similar decisions in the future, aiming for a more balanced or effective strategy.

8. **Create a Feedback Loop**: Draw an arrow leading back to the top of the page, symbolizing the application of these insights to future financial decisions.

9. **Repeat for Other Decisions**: Use this flowchart method for other financial decisions to build a more comprehensive understanding of your decision-making patterns.

Purpose

Creating this flowchart will help you visually dissect and understand the complexities of your financial decision-making. By recognizing the roles of both emotional and rational factors, you can work towards more balanced and effective financial strategies in the future. This activity promotes deeper self-awareness in financial matters, aligning with the principles discussed in the chapter.

Twelve

SURPRISE!

CHAPTER SUMMARY

In Chapter 12, Morgan Housel discusses the complex relationship between historical financial events and future economic forecasting. He emphasizes that while history is valuable for setting expectations and understanding common mistakes, it is not reliable for predicting future economic outcomes. This is mainly due to the unpredictable nature of human emotions, which play a significant role in investment decisions and market dynamics.

Housel points out the risks of over-reliance on historical financial data, cautioning against the fallacy of treating historians as prophets. He highlights that major historical events like the Great Depression, World War II, the dot-com bubble, and the mid-2000s housing crisis have profoundly impacted the world and the economy. Often outliers in historical data, these events demonstrate how rapidly situations can escalate and change.

He further explains that the global economy often hinges on unprecedented events. While we tend to use past occurrences like the Great Depression and World War II to guide our future investment decisions, this approach is more a failure of imagination than of analysis. The most significant future economic events will likely be those that history provides little guidance for, leaving us unprepared due to their unprecedented nature. Housel suggests that the key lesson from historical shocks is the inherent unpredictability and complexity of the world.

Additionally, Housel argues that historical analysis can be misleading when forecasting the economy's and stock markets' future. This is because it does not consider critical structural changes in today's world. He cites the rise of 401(k) plans, the advent of venture capital, and the increasing intervals between recessions as examples of such significant changes.

Referencing Benjamin Graham's "The Intelligent Investor," Housel acknowledges the book's practical advice for investors. However, he notes that many of Graham's formulas, frequently revised between 1934 and 1972, have become outdated and are no longer effective. This is attributed to the evolution of opportunities, the increased accessibility of information through technology, and the shift from an industrial to a technology-driven economy. These changes have heightened competition and altered the financial landscape.

Housel concludes by asserting that while the study of monetary history can offer general insights, relying on it to predict specific patterns, trades, sectors, and causal links manifests evolution in action. He reiterates that historians are not prophets and stresses the importance of planning for the future with an understanding that history offers guidance but is not a definitive predictor.

KEY TAKEAWAYS

1. **History as a Misleading Guide**: While economic and investment history is valuable for understanding patterns and tendencies, it often fails to predict future events accurately due to the unprecedented nature of major economic shifts.

2. **The Fallacy of "Historians as Prophets"**: There's a common misconception that past financial data and events can reliably predict future conditions, ignoring the constant evolution and innovation in the financial world.

3. **Impact of Human Emotions**: Financial markets are not just driven by hard data but also by the emotions and behaviors of investors, making predictions based on historical data alone unreliable.

4. **The Role of Surprises in Economics**: The most significant economic impacts often come from unpredictable, outlier events, demonstrating the limitations of historical data in forecasting.

5. **Evolving Economic Landscapes**: The ever-changing nature of economies and markets, including technological advancements and consumer preference shifts, challenges past data's applicability to future scenarios.

REFLECTIVE QUESTIONS

Personal Experience with Financial Surprises: Reflect when a financial or economic event surprised you. How did this event challenge your previous understanding or expectations based on historical data?

_____

_____

_____

_____

_____

_____

Adapting to Unpredictability: Considering the unpredictable nature of financial markets, how might you approach financial planning or investing differently? What strategies could you use to prepare for unforeseen economic changes?

_____

_____

_____

_____

_____

_____

ACTIVITY: "THE FUTURE FORECAST CHALLENGE"

Objective

Design a creative activity that challenges conventional financial forecasting and planning thinking, emphasizing adaptability and readiness for surprises.

Instructions

1. **Create a 'Future Scenarios' Chart**: Develop a chart with two columns: "Predictable Trends" and "Potential Surprises". Under "Predictable Trends," list economic patterns or trends you believe are likely to continue based on historical data. In the "Potential Surprises" column, brainstorm unexpected events or changes that could significantly impact the economy or your personal finances.

2. **Develop Response Strategies**: For each potential surprise, devise a strategy or plan to adapt to that scenario, focusing on flexibility and resilience.

3. **Assess Your Preparedness**: Evaluate your current financial plan or investment strategy in light of these potential surprises. Identify areas where you could improve your preparedness for unexpected economic changes.

4. **Reflect on Learning**: Consider how this exercise has altered your perception of financial forecasting and the importance of being prepared for the unpredictable.

Purpose

This activity fosters a more dynamic and adaptable approach to financial planning, encouraging you to think beyond historical trends and prepare for the twists and turns of economic and investment landscapes.

Thirteen

ROOM FOR ERROR

CHAPTER SUMMARY

Morgan Housel explores the concept of card counting practiced by blackjack players in Las Vegas casinos, using it as a metaphor for effective money management. This technique involves tracking the cards that have been dealt to estimate the likelihood of certain cards being drawn by the dealer. Players bet more when the odds are in their favor and less when they're not. While card counting can tilt the odds slightly toward the player, it's crucial to recognize that excessive betting can be risky, even under favorable odds. The key lesson here is acknowledging uncertainty, randomness, and the constant presence of chance in life. This understanding aligns with Benjamin Graham's 'margin of safety' principle, a concept central to managing in a world governed by probabilities rather than certainties. Housel notes that this margin for error is often underestimated in financial matters, even by experts like stock analysts and economic forecasters. When appropriately utilized, a margin for error provides resilience and the ability to capitalize on low-probability, high-impact events.

According to Housel, investors should incorporate a margin for error in their strategies, particularly concerning market volatility, retirement savings, and optimism bias in risk-taking. While spreadsheets and models can estimate future returns, they fail to accurately account for the emotional and financial impacts of those returns. To counteract this, Housel suggests investors assume future returns will be lower than historical averages – for example, 13 percent less – as a margin of safety.

This approach offers a more realistic perspective on potential outcomes. Additionally, he highlights the danger of optimism bias in risk-taking, which often leads to an overemphasis on favorable outcomes while neglecting significant downsides. Similarly, using leverage can mask the true probability of failure, causing a consistent undervaluation of risks.

Housel emphasizes the critical importance of avoiding single points of failure in life, such as relying solely on a paycheck for short-term financial needs. This reliance can lead to complicated situations like unexpected emergencies or job losses. To mitigate these risks, it's advised to avoid depending solely on regular income for immediate expenses and save for unforeseen costs instead. Housel also advocates saving for unpredictable and incomprehensible future events, as crucial as saving for specific goals like a car, house, or retirement. Assuming that one can predict future expenses presupposes a level of certainty that doesn't exist. He argues that the most essential part of any financial plan is to prepare for the unexpected, acknowledging that things often do not go as planned.

KEY TAKEAWAYS

1. **Card Counting and Financial Planning**: The strategy of blackjack card counters, who bet more when odds favor them and less when they don't, parallels the need for caution and flexibility in financial planning.

2. **Margin of Safety**: Benjamin Graham's concept of a margin of safety is pivotal; it implies that preparing for a range of outcomes is more prudent than relying on precise forecasts.

3. **Overconfidence in Historical Data**: Relying too heavily on historical financial data can lead to overconfidence and a lack of preparedness for unprecedented events.

4. **Unpredictability of Markets**: Financial markets are influenced by unique and unforeseen events, making it crucial to have a plan accommodating unexpected changes.

5. **Avoiding Ruin**: The primary goal in financial management should be to avoid decisions that could lead to complete financial ruin, regardless of potential gains.

REFLECTIVE QUESTIONS

Applying Card Counting to Finances: How can the principles of card counting in blackjack apply to your personal financial strategy? Are there areas where you could improve your approach to risk?

Planning for the Unpredictable: Reflect on a past financial decision that didn't go as planned. How could having a greater margin of safety or room for error have changed the outcome?

Fourteen

You'll Change

Chapter Summary

Morgan Housel recounts a story from his youth about a friend who, despite facing considerable obstacles, fulfilled his lifelong dream of becoming a doctor. This story highlights the importance of acknowledging realistic life circumstances and the impact of unrealistic financial aspirations on future financial planning. This scenario is not uncommon; only about 27% of college graduates end up working in a field related to their major. While long-term financial planning is essential, making such plans is complicated because our perceptions of what we want in the future are likely to evolve.

Housel discusses the 'End of History Illusion,' a psychological phenomenon where people recognize the changes they have undergone in the past but often underestimate how much they will change in the future. This tendency can significantly affect long-term financial goals, as people frequently do not anticipate how much their circumstances and desires might shift. To avoid future regrets and the adverse effects of compounding mistakes, Housel advises avoiding extremes in financial planning. Focusing on maintaining balance in annual savings, leisure time, commute, and family time can help manage expectations and foster endurance. He emphasizes the importance of acknowledging the possibility of changing one's mind and moving swiftly to minimize future regret.

Housel points out that sunk costs and decisions based on past efforts that cannot be recovered are particularly detrimental in a world where personal growth and change are constant. He advises that financial goals, especially those set by external influences, should be reconsidered and, if necessary, abandoned without remorse. This approach can help mitigate future regret and prevent the compounding of ineffective financial strategies.

KEY TAKEAWAYS

1. **Embrace Flexibility in Financial Planning**: Recognizing that personal aspirations and situations can change, the author implies that financial plans should be revisited and adjusted periodically to reflect current goals and circumstances.

2. **Avoid Extremes in Planning**: The chapter suggests avoiding overly rigid financial strategies that might not accommodate future changes. This includes not committing to extreme lifestyles or financial goals that may become unsuitable or cause regret later in life.

3. **Let Go of Sunk Costs**: The author hints at the importance of not being anchored by past financial decisions, especially when they no longer align with current or future needs. This involves abandoning outdated plans or investments to make room for more relevant choices.

4. **Plan for Different Life Stages**: The underlying message is to consider how your financial needs and goals might change at different life stages and plan accordingly rather than sticking to a static plan made at a younger age.

5. **Regular Review of Financial Goals**: The discussion implies that individuals should regularly reassess their financial goals and plans, ensuring they remain aligned with evolving personal circumstances and aspirations.

REFLECTIVE QUESTIONS

Personal Evolution and Financial Plans: Reflect on how your goals and aspirations have changed. How have these changes affected your financial planning and decisions?

Adapting to Future Changes: How can you incorporate flexibility into your current financial plan to accommodate potential changes in your future preferences, goals, or circumstances?

ACTIVITY: "THE EVOLVING GOALS TIMELINE" USING ONLINE TOOLS

Objective

Create a personalized timeline to continuously reassess and adapt your financial goals in alignment with life's changes using online timeline creation tools.

Recommended Online Tools

1. **Canva Timeline Maker:** Canva offers an intuitive, drag-and-drop timeline creator with various design options. It's user-friendly and allows for creative customization of your timeline.

2. **Visme:** Visme offers a basic free plan that includes timeline creation. While more advanced features may require a paid plan, the free version is comprehensive for basic needs.

3. **Creately:** Creately allows for easy creation of timelines with its free plan, though it may have limitations on features and the number of diagrams you can create.

4. **Preceden Timeline Maker:** Preceden offers a free version with basic timeline-making capabilities. It's suitable for simple, linear timelines.

5. **Adobe Express:** Adobe Express provides free access to timeline creation tools, though some advanced features may be limited to the premium version.

Instructions

1. **Choose Your Timeline Tool:** Select one of the recommended online tools: Canva Timeline Maker, Visme, Creately, Preceden Timeline Maker, or Adobe Express. Each tool offers a user-friendly interface and customizable templates.

2. **Set Up Your Timeline**:

- ○ Create a new timeline project in your chosen tool.

- ○ Customize the timeline to represent different stages of your life, from young adulthood to retirement. Mark the timeline in 5-year intervals.

3. **Past and Present Goals Assessment**:

- ○ For past life stages, use the tool's features to add notes or markers indicating your primary financial goals and aspirations during each period.

- ○ Reflect on your current financial goals and add them to your current age on the timeline.

4. **Future Goals Projection**:

- ○ Project your potential future goals at each future interval. Consider possible life changes like career shifts, family dynamics, or retirement plans.

- ○ Use the tool's features to highlight these projections, possibly with different colors or symbols, to denote varying levels of certainty.

5. **Schedule Regular Reviews**: In the tool, set reminders or markers at specific intervals (e.g., every five years) for revisiting and potentially revising your goals to adapt to life changes.

6. **Save and Revisit**:

- ○ Save your timeline project in the tool. Many of these tools offer cloud storage, allowing you to access and update your timeline from anywhere.

- ○ Set external reminders in your calendar to revisit your timeline regularly for updates and adjustments.

Purpose

This activity leverages the capabilities of online tools to make tracking and updating financial goals over different life stages more efficient and visually engaging. By regularly revisiting and updating the timeline, you'll ensure that your financial planning adapts to your evolving life circumstances and aspirations.

Outcome

You'll have a dynamic, easily accessible, and visually appealing timeline that reflects your current financial goals and is adaptable to future changes. This approach fosters a flexible and proactive attitude toward financial planning, crucial for accommodating life's inevitable evolutions.

Fifteen

NOTHING'S FREE

CHAPTER SUMMARY

Chapter 15 emphasizes the vital understanding of success's price and the willingness to bear it. It reflects on the 2008 financial crisis and the downfall of General Electric, once at the pinnacle of global corporations. This backdrop illustrates the complexities financial players encounter, from juggling stakeholder and regulatory demands to the challenge of keeping a long-term view amidst market crashes.

Housel conveys that investing successfully incurs more than financial costs. It involves navigating the emotional and psychological terrain of fear, doubt, volatility, uncertainty, and regret. Investors are encouraged to acknowledge these aspects as integral to the process, understanding that significant returns require accepting market volatility, engaging with less uncertain assets, or balancing the pursuit of returns with tolerance for volatility.

A study by Morningstar on tactical mutual funds is cited, showing a half percent annual underperformance due to frequent trading rather than adhering to a buy-and-hold strategy. This exemplifies a common dilemma where investors seek to avoid the genuine cost of sound investment returns. The chapter suggests reinterpreting market volatility as a 'fee' rather than a punitive 'fine,' helping investors develop the resilience and patience necessary for long-term gains.

The chapter asserts that market returns are inherently tied to a volatility/uncertainty 'fee.' This 'fee' is the entry price for potential returns exceeding those of lower-risk options like cash and bonds. The narrative urges investors to see this 'fee' not merely as a tolerable aspect but as a valuable investment for future rewards.

KEY TAKEAWAYS

1. **The Hidden Price of Success**: Success, particularly in the financial realm, always has a price, which is often not apparent until it's time to pay up.

2. **The Misconceptions of Wealth**: The chapter uses the example of General Electric's fall to illustrate how appearances of success can be misleading and how actual costs can emerge unexpectedly.

3. **Investment Requires Enduring Volatility**: Successful investing is portrayed not just as a matter of strategy but also of enduring the inherent volatility and uncertainty of the market.

4. **Volatility as an Investment Fee**: The chapter argues that market volatility should be viewed as a fee rather than a fine, a necessary cost for the potential gains over time.

5. **Realizing and Accepting Investment Costs**: Acknowledging and accepting the cost of investment (volatility and emotional stress) is crucial for long-term success in the financial world.

REFLECTIVE QUESTIONS

Recognizing Investment Costs: Reflect on your experiences with investing or financial decision-making. How have you perceived and handled the inherent costs, like market volatility or emotional stress?

_____

_____

_____

_____

_____

_____

_____

_____

Changing Perspectives on Financial Risks: How might viewing market volatility and investment risks as necessary fees rather than penalties change your investing and financial planning approach?

_____

_____

_____

_____

_____

_____

_____

Sixteen

YOU & ME

CHAPTER SUMMARY

The dot-com and housing bubbles, causing significant financial setbacks, wiped out household wealth by approximately $6.2 trillion and $8 trillion, respectively. A common interpretation attributes these events to greed, yet this oversimplification overlooks the reality that people often make regrettable financial decisions with limited information and a lack of logical reasoning. The intricacies of learning from bubbles are compounded by intense competition for investment returns and the ambiguous attribution of cause and blame. Financial bubbles often stem from investors relying on cues from others, who may have different investment strategies, rather than on fundamental analysis. This herd mentality can lead to inflated asset values, creating bubbles when short-term gains draw substantial investment, altering the dynamics of market price setting.

The dot-com and housing bubbles were marked by an irrational optimism about the future, with many investors fixating on short-term trades and options. This environment fostered speculative bubbles, characterized by rational engagement in short-term trading to capitalize on the momentum that had become self-sustaining. In this climate, pursuing profits overshadowed traditional long-term investment strategies, especially regarding asset valuation. Problems arose when long-term investors, adhering to one set of principles, began mimicking the tactics of short-term traders, who operated under a different set of rules. An example of this was the surge in Cisco's stock, which rose by 300% in 1999 to $60 per share, drawing in long-term investors at what appeared to be reasonable prices.

Investment decisions in finance are frequently influenced by observing and reacting to the actions of others, yet it's crucial to recognize that different investors have varying goals and perspectives. Rising prices can lure value-conscious investors into an unrealistic optimism. Investors must understand their time horizons and resist being swayed by those engaged in different investment "games." Identifying one's investment strategy and not being influenced by the actions of others is critical. Moreover, pessimism can significantly impact investment choices, further complicating decision-making.

Key Takeaways

1. **Inherent Complexity of Bubbles**: Financial bubbles are complex events influenced by multiple factors, making them difficult to predict or prevent.

2. **Diverse Investor Motivations**: Different investors have varying goals and time horizons, leading to different perceptions of value and rationality in financial decisions.

3. **Impact of Short-Term Traders**: The influence of short-term traders can often skew market perceptions, leading to misalignments between price and long-term value.

4. **Misinterpretation of Market Signals**: Long-term investors can be misled by the actions of short-term traders, mistaking market momentum for sustainable growth.

5. **Recognizing Your Investment Game**: Identifying and understanding your investment goals and strategies is crucial to navigating financial markets and avoiding the pitfalls of bubble dynamics.

REFLECTIVE QUESTIONS

Personal Reaction to Market Trends: How do you typically react to significant market movements or trends? Do you consider the different motivations behind these movements before making investment decisions?

_____

_____

_____

_____

_____

_____

_____

Understanding Your Investment Strategy: Reflect on your investment strategy. How does it align or differ from the short-term trading strategies that often drive market bubbles? How can you ensure that you stay true to your plan amidst market volatility?

_____

_____

_____

_____

_____

_____

_____

Seventeen

THE SEDUCTION OF PESSIMISM

CHAPTER SUMMARY

Morgan Housel highlights the contrast between optimism and pessimism in financial perspectives. Optimism, he notes, is the belief that the world will generally get better for most people, while pessimism, often seen as more intellectually compelling, is more widespread. Optimism rests on the idea that most people strive for improvement rather than creating problems.

Reflecting on 2008, Housel recalls the economic turmoil that marked it as one of the worst years in recent history, with plummeting stock markets and soaring unemployment rates. The Wall Street Journal featured a front-page article about Russian academic Igor Panarin's prediction that the U.S. would disintegrate into six parts by the end of 2010, with Alaska returning to Russian control. This type of pessimistic outlook, often seen as apocalyptic, is not uncommon in history, where countries have indeed fallen apart. However, Housel points out pessimism often appears more intelligent and plausible than optimism, overshadowing success stories. The investment newsletter industry, for example, has long been dominated by doomsayers despite the stock market's substantial growth over the past century.

Pessimism, particularly in financial matters, has an intuitive and unavoidable allure. This is partly due to loss aversion, an evolutionary trait where the emphasis on risk over opportunity enhances survival and reproduction chances. Financial pessimism often seems more compelling than optimism because money is a pervasive concern, and the stock market, a frequent topic in media, exacerbates this worry. However, narratives focused on downturns simplify the creation of future predictions, overlooking the market's ability to adapt. The 2008 spike in oil prices is an example, where new fracking and horizontal drilling techniques eventually led to a significant increase in oil production by 2019. Pessimists often fail to consider such adaptations, leading to a linear view of economic forecasts.

Progress is typically slow and often overshadowed by rapid setbacks. The invention of the airplane by the Wright Brothers is used as an example. Initially, the airplane was misunderstood and underestimated, seen merely as a military weapon, a luxury for the rich, or a novel mode of transport. This contrasts with the immediate attention to adverse events like corporate failures, large-scale wars, and aviation disasters. The gradual process of compounding drives growth, while destruction often results from single incidents that erode trust. In medicine, for instance, the age-adjusted death rate from cardiac disease has significantly decreased since the 1960s, a testament to slow but steady progress. In investing, understanding the balance between the costs of success, such as volatility and losses, against a backdrop of long-term growth is crucial. The chapter concludes that while expecting positive outcomes might seem unremarkable, pessimism sets a lower bar, narrowing the gap between expectations and reality.

KEY TAKEAWAYS

1. **Pessimism's Intellectual Appeal**: Pessimism, especially in financial contexts, often appears more sophisticated and realistic than optimism, drawing more attention and consideration.

2. **Definition of Optimism in Finance**: True optimism is not only expecting positive outcomes but also believing in favorable odds over time and acknowledging setbacks.

3. **The Asymmetry of Attention**: Negative financial events and predictions typically receive more attention and are easier to articulate than positive ones, skewing public perception towards pessimism.

4. **The Slow Progress of Optimism**: Optimistic developments in finance often occur gradually and go unnoticed, whereas pessimistic events are usually sudden and garner immediate attention.

5. **The Power of Reduced Expectations**: Pessimism can lower expectations, making any positive outcome feel surprisingly good, which ironically can lead to a form of optimism.

REFLECTIVE QUESTIONS

Your Financial Outlook: How do you typically approach financial news and predictions? Do you find yourself more influenced by pessimistic or optimistic viewpoints?

_____

_____

_____

_____

_____

_____

Balancing Pessimism and Optimism: Reflect on a financial decision you made in the past. How did your outlook, whether pessimistic or optimistic, affect that decision? With hindsight, would a balanced view have led to a different choice?

_____

_____

_____

_____

_____

_____

_____

Eighteen

WHEN YOU'LL BELIEVE ANYTHING

CHAPTER SUMMARY

An intriguing scenario is presented where an alien observer studies Earth's economy during the 2007 to 2009 period. The observer notes the unchanged aspects of population, technology, and institutions, yet a stark contrast in the economic wellbeing of US families, who were $16 trillion poorer in 2009 than in 2007. This paradox is attributed to the powerful stories we tell ourselves about the economy. The misconception that home prices would always rise led to a series of financial collapses, showing the profound impact of narratives on economic stability.

Housel highlights that this story-driven dynamic can lead to overestimations in the likelihood of certain economic beliefs being true, which is detrimental to personal financial management. Investment strategies, influenced by narratives and predictions with slim chances of accuracy, can be enticing yet misleading. The disparity between what one wishes to be accurate and what needs to be true for a favorable outcome can lead to vulnerability to financial myths.

The chapter then explores how our limited understanding shapes our perception of the world. Just as children struggle to grasp concepts like budgeting and savings, adults also interpret the world through their limited range of experiences. This can result in errors across various domains. Often based on these limited perspectives, market forecasting is frequently incorrect, yet it continues to be in high demand.

Housel points out that people often seek control in an unpredictable world and are drawn to authoritative figures promising certainty. This tendency can lead to misunderstandings in interpreting complex situations like those in economics and finance. It encourages overconfidence in personal opinions and a disregard for the roles of chance and external factors. Acknowledging our limited perspective is crucial for making more informed and realistic decisions, especially in business and financial planning.

KEY TAKEAWAYS

1. **Narrative-Driven Economy**: The chapter emphasizes that the economy is heavily influenced by the stories and narratives we create and believe rather than just tangible assets and capabilities.

2. **Perception vs. Reality**: A significant point is that our perception of economic conditions can vastly differ from the actual physical and technological advancements present, as seen through the lens of an observing alien.

3. **Impact of Changing Narratives**: The shift in economic narratives, particularly during crises, can lead to substantial economic changes, as seen in the contrast between 2007 and 2009.

4. **The Power of Belief**: The chapter underscores how belief in certain economic narratives, even if not based on concrete facts, can profoundly affect the economy.

5. **Stories Over Facts**: It suggests compelling stories often influence more than hard financial data, affecting investment decisions and market movements.

REFLECTIVE QUESTIONS

Narrative Influence on Decisions: Consider when a prevalent economic narrative influenced your financial decision. How did the story you believed compare to the actual economic reality?

Evaluating Economic Stories: Reflect on a current economic narrative. How does it shape your perception of the economy, and what steps can you take to assess its validity critically?

ACTIVITY: NARRATIVE VS. REALITY ANALYSIS

Objective

To differentiate between economic narratives and actual economic conditions, helping you make more informed financial decisions.

Instructions

1. **Choose an Economic Narrative:** Select a familiar economic story or belief from media or discussions.

2. **Gather Facts**: Research actual economic data and conditions linked to this narrative, including financial indicators and market data.

3. **Create a Comparison Table**: Make a two-column table - one for the narrative's critical points, the other for the actual economic facts.

4. **Analyze and Reflect**: Examine the differences and similarities. Think about how the narrative might be distorting or missing essential economic realities.

Purpose

To enhance your skills in evaluating economic narratives against actual data, aiding in more informed financial decisions. This helps discern between persuasive stories and actual economic conditions, effectively navigating financial market complexities.

Nineteen

ALL TOGETHER NOW

CHAPTER SUMMARY

In the summary chapter, author Morgan Housel recounts an incident from a dentist appointment, using it as a metaphor to illustrate the complexities of financial advice. The story underscores that in 1931, consent in the doctor-patient relationship was not as clearly defined as it is now. It also points out that medical education has evolved from focusing solely on disease treatment to considering the patient's overall wellbeing. This shift parallels the role of financial advisors, who must acknowledge the influence of luck and risk in financial planning. Advisors are reminded to exercise humility when successful and to offer forgiveness and compassion when things don't go as planned, recognizing the intricate interplay of luck and risk.

Housel emphasizes that wealth accumulation involves deferring immediate gratification for future benefits. He advises that effective wealth management includes strategies that ensure peace of mind, extend one's financial planning horizon, and be prepared for various outcomes. He suggests using wealth to gain more control over personal time, advocating for kindness and modesty over ostentation. Preparing for unforeseen and indefinable future events is also crucial. He advises defining the personal cost of achieving success and allowing a margin of error in financial decisions. Other key points include avoiding extreme financial strategies, balancing risk with caution against catastrophic losses, understanding the specific financial game one is playing, and embracing the inherent messiness of financial planning. Housel stresses that there is no universal solution in finance; the key lies in understanding and respecting individuals' diverse goals and desires.

KEY TAKEAWAYS

1. **Personalized Financial Decision-Making**: Emphasizes the importance of understanding individual financial goals and circumstances, similar to how modern medicine focuses on patient-specific treatments.

2. **Universal Financial Truths**: Acknowledges that while personalization is critical, there are universal truths in finance that everyone can apply.

3. **Critical Recommendations for Financial Health**:

   - **Balance Humility and Compassion**: Recognize the roles of luck and risk, and don't overestimate personal control over financial outcomes.

   - **Ego vs. Wealth**: Understand that wealth accumulation involves managing one's desires and ego.

   - **Comfort Over Returns**: Make financial decisions that ensure personal comfort and peace of mind.

   - **Embrace Long-Term Investing**: Recognize the power of time in investing for substantial growth.

   - **Acceptance of Failures**: Be comfortable with investments not always succeeding; focus on overall portfolio performance.

   - **Time Over Money**: Value time as a critical aspect of happiness and use money to control and enjoy your time.

- **Prioritize Kindness Over Materialism**: Focus on earning respect through humility rather than material possessions.

- **The Importance of Saving**: Save regularly without a specific purpose as a buffer for life's unpredictability.

- **Understanding the Cost of Success**: Be prepared to face the non-monetary costs (like uncertainty and regret) in financial endeavors.

- **Room for Error**: Maintain a buffer in financial plans to accommodate unforeseen events.

- **Avoid Financial Extremes**: Keep financial decisions moderate to adapt to changing life situations.

- **Risk Management**: Balance taking risks for growth and avoiding catastrophic risks.

- **Define Your Financial Game**: Be aware of your financial goals, and do not let others influence you with different objectives.

- **Embrace Complexity and Diversity**: Accept that finance isn't one-size-fits-all and that different approaches can be valid.

Twenty

CONFESSIONS

CHAPTER SUMMARY

Sandy Gottesman, a renowned billionaire investor, often probes job candidates about how they manage their personal finances. This approach underscores the disparity between people's words and financial behaviors. According to Morningstar, nearly half of all US mutual fund portfolio managers do not invest their own money in the funds they manage. This trend of professionals making different choices for themselves compared to what they recommend is not isolated to finance. It's seen in other fields, such as medicine, where doctors might choose different end-of-life treatments for themselves than their patients. These examples highlight that there's no universal answer to complex and sensitive issues. Financial decisions are often influenced by personal dynamics, like the desire to avoid disappointing family members during conversations at the dinner table.

Morgan Housel, a financial writer and analyst, exemplifies a conservative approach to personal finance. He and his wife lead a modest lifestyle, prioritizing living within their means and valuing independence over material wealth. Their financial choices, which may appear unconventional, include owning their home outright without a mortgage and keeping a significant portion of their assets in cash. This strategy stems from their desire for independence and an aversion to the social pressure of 'keeping up with the Joneses.' They regard money as vital to maintaining financial freedom, as it eliminates the need to liquidate investments for unexpected expenses. Housel's perspective on personal finance centers on being prepared for life's unpredictability, which he views as more critical than saving for specific high-value purchases.

In his investment journey, Housel transitioned from holding a portfolio of 25 individual stocks to investing in a low-cost index fund. He advocates that each investor should adopt the strategy that best suits their likelihood of success. He supports the concept of dollar-cost averaging into a low-cost index fund to enhance the chances of long-term investment success. Housel asserts that there isn't necessarily a correlation between the investment effort and the outcomes achieved. The global economy, he believes, is influenced by rare but impactful events. Therefore, simple investment strategies can be effective, provided they capture the key elements crucial to success. Housel's overarching financial objective is achieving independence and mastering the psychology of money, which he acknowledges is unique to each individual.

Key Takeaways

1. **Personalized Financial Decisions**: The importance of customizing financial strategies to individual needs and circumstances rather than blindly following generic advice.

2. **Pursuit of Independence**: The primary financial goal is achieving independence, not necessarily accumulating wealth. This is achieved through maintaining a high savings rate and managing lifestyle expectations.

3. **Simplicity in Investment**: The author advocates for simplicity in investment strategies, favoring index funds for their long-term effectiveness and alignment with personal risk tolerance.

4. **Balance and Comfort**: Financial decisions should be balanced and comfortable, avoiding extremes and prioritizing peace of mind over maximizing returns.

REFLECTIVE QUESTIONS

Alignment with Personal Values:

- Reflect on your own financial goals. How do they align with the principles of independence and comfort highlighted in the chapter?

- Consider how your current financial strategies mirror or differ from those described. Can you make adjustments to better align with your values and goals?

WORKBOOK: THE PSYCHOLOGY OF MONEY

Risk Tolerance and Investment Choices:

- Assess your risk tolerance. How does this impact your investment choices?

- Evaluate the simplicity or complexity of your investment strategy. Could simplifying your approach lead to greater peace of mind or better alignment with your financial goals?

ACTIVITY: CRAFTING YOUR FINANCIAL CONFESSION - FINAL WORKBOOK ACTIVITY

Objective

To create a personal financial statement that reflects your unique goals, strategies, and values, inspired by the principles outlined in "Chapter 20: Confessions."

Instructions

1. **Personal Goal Setting**: Identify your primary financial goals, such as independence, wealth accumulation, or security.

2. **Financial Strategy Development**: Based on your goals, outline your current financial strategies. Include savings plans, investment choices, and risk management approaches.

3. **Self-Reflection**: Reflect on the alignment between your strategies and your goals. Are there discrepancies or areas for improvement?

4. **Action Plan Creation**: Develop a plan to adjust your financial strategies to better align with your personal goals and values.

5. **Continuous Review**: Commit to regularly reviewing and updating your financial confession to adapt to life changes and evolving goals.

Purpose

As the final task in this workbook, this activity encourages you to introspectively assess your financial strategies and align them with your personal goals and values. By crafting your financial confession, you create a guiding document that aids in making financial decisions that are true to your personal philosophy.

Dear Reader

Before we reach our journey's conclusion, if you found value in this workbook and feel it has positively influenced your journey, please consider sharing your experience by leaving a review on Amazon. It only takes a few minutes, and we would immensely appreciate your feedback at Jackrabbit Press. Doing so also helps others discover and benefit from these insights. To leave a review, simply scan the QR code here:

Thank you for allowing this workbook to be a part of your journey to financial freedom and enlightenment.

The Team at Jackrabbit Press

Postscript: A Brief History of Why the U.S. Consumer Thinks the Way They Do

Overview

In this final chapter, Morgan Housel offers a comprehensive exploration of the American consumer's mindset, tracing its origins back to the post-World War II period. The chapter illuminates the significant economic and social changes that have profoundly influenced consumer attitudes toward spending, saving, and wealth accumulation.

Author's Narrative Style

Housel's eloquence shines through as he narrates the transformation of economic landscapes and their impacts on consumer behavior. He skillfully connects historical events with personal finance, underscoring the unpredictable nature of economic progress and the evolution of consumer expectations.

Reading Recommendation

Due to Morgan Housel's exceptional storytelling ability, reading the entire postscript is highly recommended to appreciate fully the intricacies and insights he presents. A summary would not capture the depth and nuances Housel brings to this narrative. He offers a rich context for understanding today's financial behaviors and attitudes, deeply rooted in historical events.

Reflective Thought

"History is just one damned thing after another." This line perfectly summarizes the chapter's essence – the relentless flow of events that continually shape our world and perceptions, particularly in personal finance. Housel encourages readers to consider the broader historical context that influences our financial decisions, moving beyond surface-level economic trends.

Morgan Housel's adept storytelling and thorough analysis make this postscript essential reading for anyone interested in the complexities of personal finance and consumer behavior seen through the lens of history.

Resources

Housel, Morgan. *The Psychology of Money: Timeless Lessons on Wealth, Greed, and Happiness*. Kindle ed., Harriman House, 2020. A m a z o n , www.amazon.com/Psychology-Money-Timeless-lessons-happiness-ebook/dp/B084HJSJJ2/ref=sr_1_1.

"4 Lessons I Learned From 'The Psychology of Money' by Morgan Housel." Business Insider, www.businessinsider.com/personal-finance/lessons-psychology-of-money-morgan-housel-2021-2?r=US&IR=T.

Weatherburn, Chris. "The Psychology of Money by Morgan Housel." ChrisWeatherburn.com, chrisweatherburn.com/the-psychology-of-money-by-morgan-housel/.

"Market Perspective." PGWM, www.pgwm.net/single-post/market-perspective.

"The Psychology of Money - Morgan Housel - Book Notes and Takeaways." Arrowpoint Wealth, arrowpointwealth.com/the-psychology-of-money-morgan-housel-book-notes-and-takeaways/.

Made in the USA
Las Vegas, NV
02 July 2024